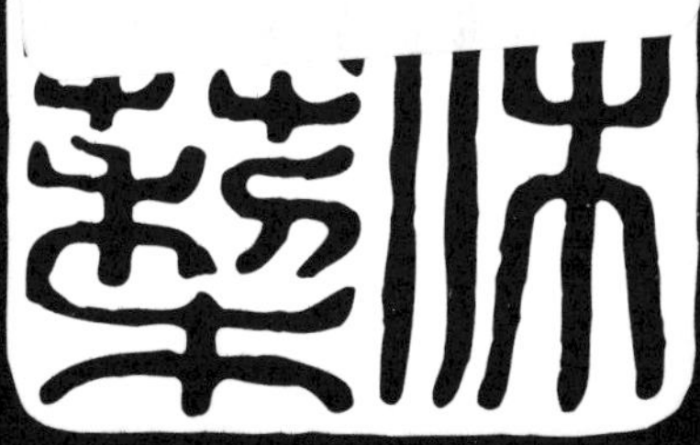

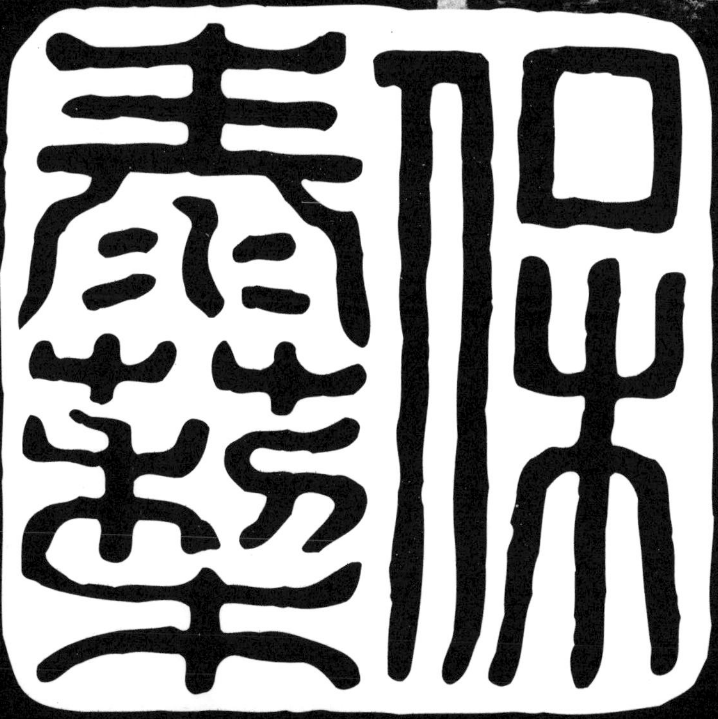

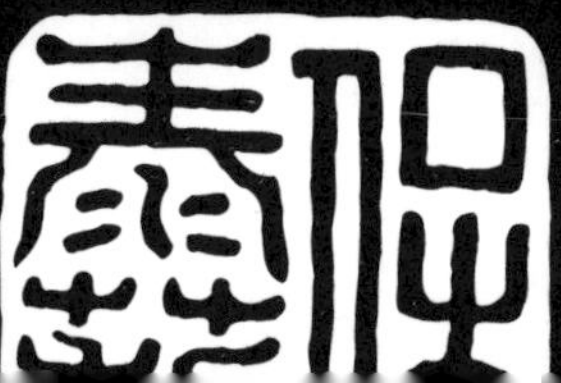

NATHALIE HAMBRO

THE ART OF THE HANDBAG

A CONTEMPORARY COLLECTION

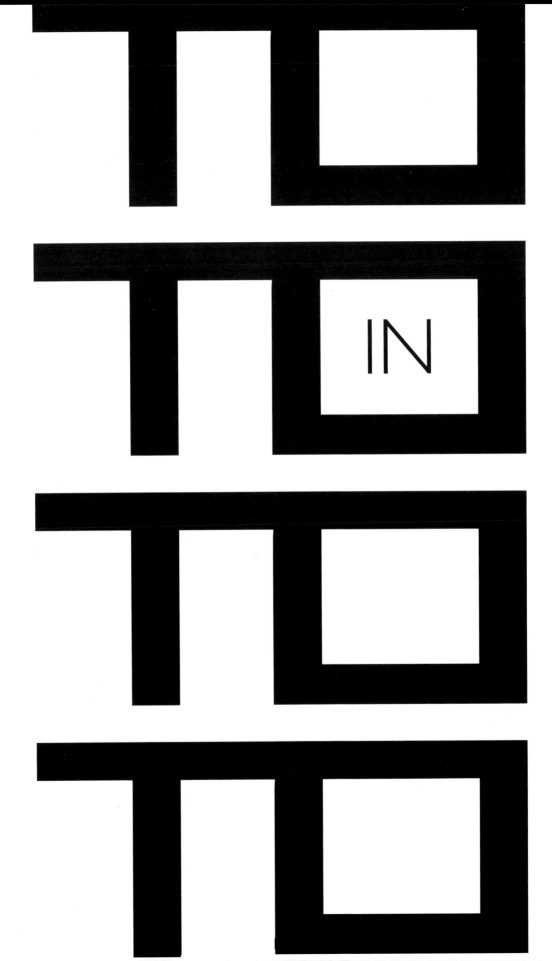

THE ART of the HANDBAG

Nathalie Hambro's designs are unique: neither a reflection of passing fashions nor, a product of theories in vogue, they are the result of an entirely independent pursuit of the eclectic. She has taken the old criteria for measuring worth – beauty of form, perfection of workmanship and value of material – and enriched them with her very precise sense of irony. Handbags now generally fall into one of three categories: the Practical, the Status Symbol and the Artwork. Nathalie Hambro produces artworks, but not at the expense of utility, and it is this dialogue between use and its expression which forms the narrative to these pieces. As more and more designers work with the cynical hindsight of the late 20th Century – through deconstruction and making the hidden process of creativity visible to an increasingly jaded public – Nathalie Hambro has rethought the language of her medium by including the boundaries of a technical intelligence. And with the same thrill of tracing a hand-stitched seam of a couture dress or the sub- structure of a Savile Row suit, each bag conjures up the presence of its creator. All good design, and particularly fashion with its obvious relation to the body, becomes a fetishistic process; one of imbuing inanimate materials with a magical or spiritual quality. The covert pleasure of sliding a hand into a hidden interior has obvious potential for an urban fetishist, and Nathalie Hambro has unquestionably mastered the art of making the product greater than the sum of its parts.

Without extrapolating from biography a formula for design, it is difficult to resist speculating on its influence. Nathalie Hambro studied at the Faculty of Law and read History of Art at l'Ecole du Louvre. She has written several cookery books, the first one of which – *Particular Delights* – addresses 'all the senses'. Before setting up her company, NMH, in 1994, she styled books, fashion and interiors, wrote for various newspapers and magazines and was a contributing editor to Vogue. A jurisprudent, epicurian, fashion arbitress? Certainly in this collection of work, the logical, the sensual and the critical each have a tangible presence.

But more revealing, perhaps, is the environment in which she lives and works; her work being a natural extension of a life in which rigorous order restrains an almost melancholy romanticism. A dimly lit entrance corridor is studded with tiny Indian mirrored discs which flash against walls as grey as thunderclouds. Black marble capitals support vases of petrified branches, while in corners, giant spools of brilliantly coloured wire gleam darkly. The series of strangely tactile, punched metal pianola discs which frame the door to her studio could serve as a metaphor for the work itself... the ethereal tattooed in steel. Inside a variety of objects are precisely positioned on or around the vast central worktable: a plaster hand in a chainmail glove; a pair of globular lead finials; a collection of glass lenses; Chinese seals and dragon-stamped calligraphy inks; feathered fishing flys; an armillary ball of barbed wire; a 1930's Maserati engine cog, and an axe head propped upright to resemble a tribal sculpture and a photomontage of an 18th century French interior gutted by fire. A catalogue from the Museum of Dog Collars is permanently open to a 16th century German example in iron. An envelope marked simply 'Dragonfly's wings' sits among the almost surgical tools for punching, piercing, riveting and drilling. Against this background is Nathalie Hambro's neatly ordered collection of her own handbags.

Handbags have the paradoxical dual role to display and conceal at once. Having evolved from the pocket, a hidden slit in the hem of a long dress, or a perfumed decolletage, they eventually became external and decorated – an extension of clothing. With their own independent identities, they still carry with them the promise of concealed mysteries. A handbag and its contents become a personal lexicon which threaten to unravel the character of its owner, giving them their power and expressive potential: they codify desire and reveal aspirations.

At first glance, the range of this collection can be perplexing for the diversity of the materials alone. But the clear link between each piece lies in the process rather than the product; in use of materials and the attention to detail. Nathalie Hambro's work leads to another place, one which is at once alien and instinctively familiar. Allusions to the ancient Japanese Noh theatre are filtered through an industrial aesthetic to sublime effect...the design doesn't diminish the source of inspiration but instead transfigures it, making it legible through a contemporary lens. This is not nostalgia, but modern life illuminated by a discreetly whispered history.

Nathalie Hambro does not design through drawings which are then passed on to a manufacturer to be interpreted, instead, she works through each stage of the production by hand, often taking the materials themselves as the starting point and allowing them to some extent dictate the design. This is immediately tangible in the sensuousness of the pieces where seemingly incompatible textures are invigorated by their proximity to each other. She aims, as she puts it, to 'glorify humble materials' and, by combining them with the precious through meticulous craftsmanship, she raises the mundane – industrial felt, nylon, carpet tape, scaffolding sheeting, horsehair, straw and PVC – to the level of haute couture. And, as in couture, every bag is hand-finished insuring that each is distinct. For *Bucket I,* Hambro uses jewellery making techniques (she was a member of the Society of Jewellery Historians and researched a book on antique paste) to articulate materials as diverse as electrical wire, hematite and pearls. She performs literal alchemy with the *Cabat Bag,* transmuting steel into gold. The juxtaposition between the industrial lacquered aluminium scales of the metal *'X' Bag* and the almost liquid gleam of the ebony, dramatise the qualities of each, while the leather cord threaded through the links of the strap differentiates between surfaces to be handled regularly and the main body of the bag.

To combine an aesthetic wit with utilitarian principles is a delicate exercise which Nathalie Hambro handles with skill. The construction of the *Trellis Bag* can just be glimpsed through the fine veil of stainless steel gauze that makes up the body. The folded and hand-pressed seams are tied together with a coloured leather cord which is knotted on the inside to resemble barbed wire and so becomes a visible metaphor for guarding precious possessions. Similarly, the metal *ÔX' Bags,* with their coats of chain mail, are exquisitely armoured against intruders.

For the horsehair *Purse Bags* the logo – a stamped, circular disc of dark, oxidised silver – has been modified to resemble the base of a shooting cartridge. On the *Pagoda Bag,* whose lacquered wooden handles support a syrupy, bronzed silk, a cord threaded through the hollowed centre of the logo transforms it into a Chinese coin. The rough ends of Russian braid used on the *Mother of Pearl PVC Bags* are finished with voluptuous blobs of dull gold or purple sealing wax – with ironic reference to its normal use as a proof of authenticity. The metal *Tassel Bag* is fastened with Chinese carved ebony beads and an enormous bronze or ruby silk tassel – itself bound with a licorice-black, leather knot. These are the hybrid offspring of industrial Occidentalism and ancient Orientalism.

Nathalie Hambro first traveled to Hong Kong through styling, and while there, a Chinese colleague rechristened her *Bo Tai Ne*, which roughly translates as 'Contained', 'Supremacy' and 'Jasmine'. She later adopted the Chinese characters for her Oriental alias as her mark. But it was the Japanese *inrₒ* or 'seal container', the most prestigious of the articles hung from the sashes of the male kimono, to which Hambro directly refers in this collection. Like those produced centuries ago, her interpretation (which she calls the *Inrₒ Bag*) is elliptical in plan and has a pair of channels through which silver rather than silk cord is threaded. A spherical bead fastens these cords, serving the same purpose as the original *ojime*. And this bag, with its embossed lead panels framing a veiled view of the interior, is as much a testimony to high craftsmanship as the *inrₒ* historically became.

Nathalie Hambro has been involved with every aspect of the design of this book, from conception to its remarkably swift execution. Since they worked for Vogue, she has collaborated with the photographer Jonathan Lovekin for over ten years, and she chose David Eldridge for his ability to transcribe her thoughts in a bold, iconographic style. Several of Nathalie Hambro's designs are now housed in the Permanent Collection of the Victoria and Albert Museum, and she is also designing handbags and jewellery for Balmain in Paris. Her circular nylon *Reel Bag*, with a silver reflective strip running its circumference and serving as the strap, has been recently acquired by the Hayward Gallery. But she has retained her independence and, liberated by her own autonomy, her work becomes a genuine encounter with the initiatives of spirit and reflection. It is Nathalie Hambro's curiously unsentimental pursuit of sensuality, with her almost Proustian allusions to art, time, memories and society, which elevates this collection beyond design: this is the *Art of the Handbag*.

Charlotte Skene-Catling.
London, September 1998

CONT

CHAPTER
STRAW & PVC
1

CHAPTER
FELT
2

ENTS

CHAPTER
4
FABRIC

CHAPTER
3
METAL

CHAPTER 4 FABRIC

CHAPTER 3 METAL

Accessorising

an outfit is the final

punctuation of our

sartorial message.

True

Elegance

is from within.

Inspiration

is totally spontaneous yet is
the result of much stored
information, often collected
over a long period, which
when reaching maturity
unfolds with fluidity from the
mind into a clear and
complete design.

STRAW
PVC

HAT bag

The idea for this design started from 60's fine straw hat bases. Chosing two different pastel shades, I placed one base inside the other and joined them together with contrasting binding. The coloured leather cords are knotted together to make the straps.

SATCHEL bag

The design derives from an eigthteen century saddle satchel. I embelished this straw bag with a hand-made, black bead tassel. The bag is assembled by hand with small rivets with a gunmetal finish. I fashioned the leather strap with a succession of love knots to resemble a chain.

EGG bag

An ostrich egg was the inspiration for this bag, as much for its proportions as for its pleasing elliptical shape.
I heat-treated to a blue tone the swiveling steel handle.

DRAWSTRING bag

For this version of the Drawstring Bag, I used straw outside with PVC of contrasting colour inside. The toggles are carved ebony.

NOH bag

For this bag I combined 50's straw and horsehair, the bold colour of the lining reminds me of Schiaparelli's trademark 'Shocking Pink' and has the same dramatic vibrancy.

MOTHER OF PEARL bag

I like this PVC because it reminds me of 40's bakelite. I lined the bag with silk dupion and used Russian braid for the straps, these are knotted at the ends, and the tips sealed with wax to avoid fraying. I used a lacquered copper logo to match the various iridescent tones of the PVC.

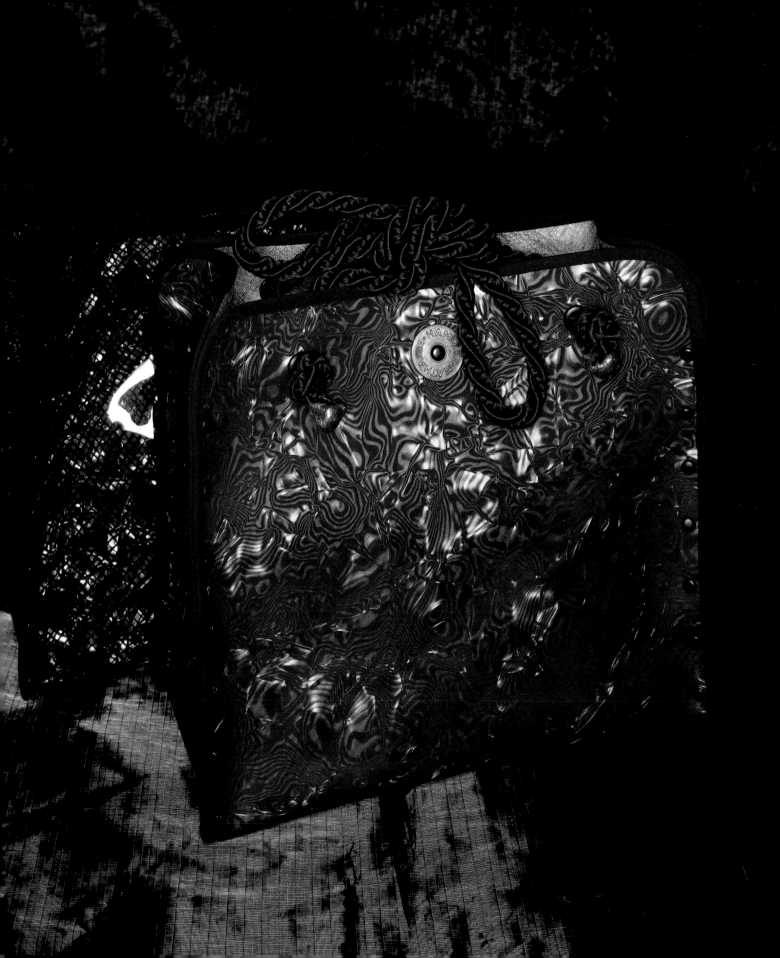

I am an intuitive designer and I

have taught myself to make

three-dimensional

samples in Kraft paper

which give me a clearer notion

for the right scale and

proportions.

FELT

TOTE bag

The tote bag is very light and roomy inside. I lashed it with tubular petersham for strength and the weight of the metal fastener - a drilled ball bearing - holds the top flap down.

BOLSTER bag

For this bag I used 100% pure wool industrial felt. I assembled it with leather cord stitching and to finish, decorated it with hand-punched perforations and rivets with a bronze finish.

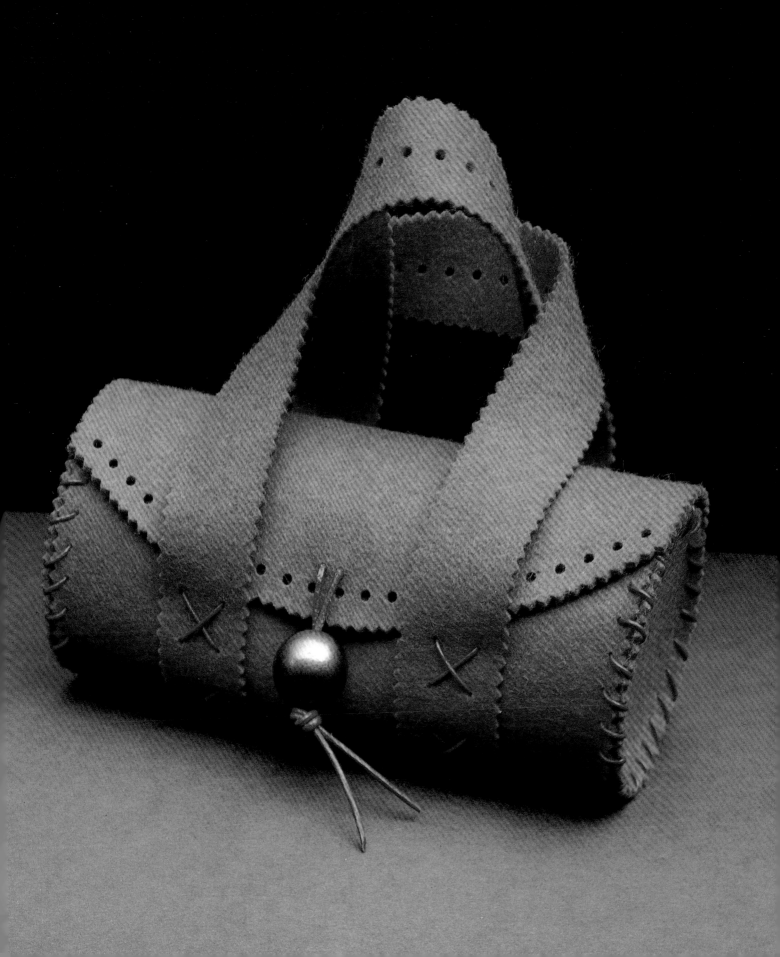

Often my initial

inspiration has a

utilitarian lineage, the design

being a kind of crystallisation of

the wisdom that comes from

everyday life.

REF H bag

I found appealing the different coloured woollen fibres in the un-dyed grey felt, as they add to the texture. The edge of the bag is boldly pinked, and the double-sided metal rivets feel as smooth inside as outside. The bag can be carried comfortably over the arm and closes with a giant industrial 'fast' link which I polished to a fine finish.

OVERNIGHT bag

This is a very large bag inspired by Joseph Beuys and Robert Morris, two artists whose work I admire. Although with an utterly different message, both used industrial felt for thought provoking sculptures and installations. The bag's straps are herringbone linen webbing.

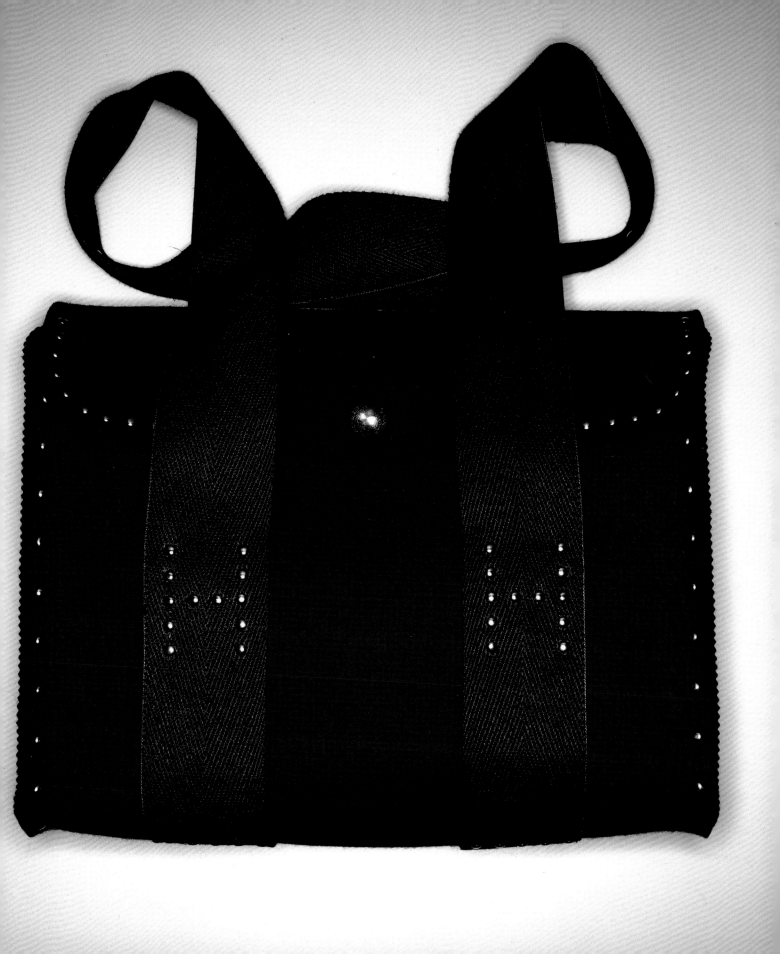

A truly **beautiful design** should be free from excess and extravagance.

I hand-craft my bags first and

foremost for myself, to satisfy a

deep sense of

work ethic.

DRAWSTRING bag

I decorated this bag using clear crystal beads tied with a leather knot. I chose the materials for their contrasting textures, the felt for its soft touch and the PVC for its shiny appearance.

Lateral thinking and cross references are part of the creative process.

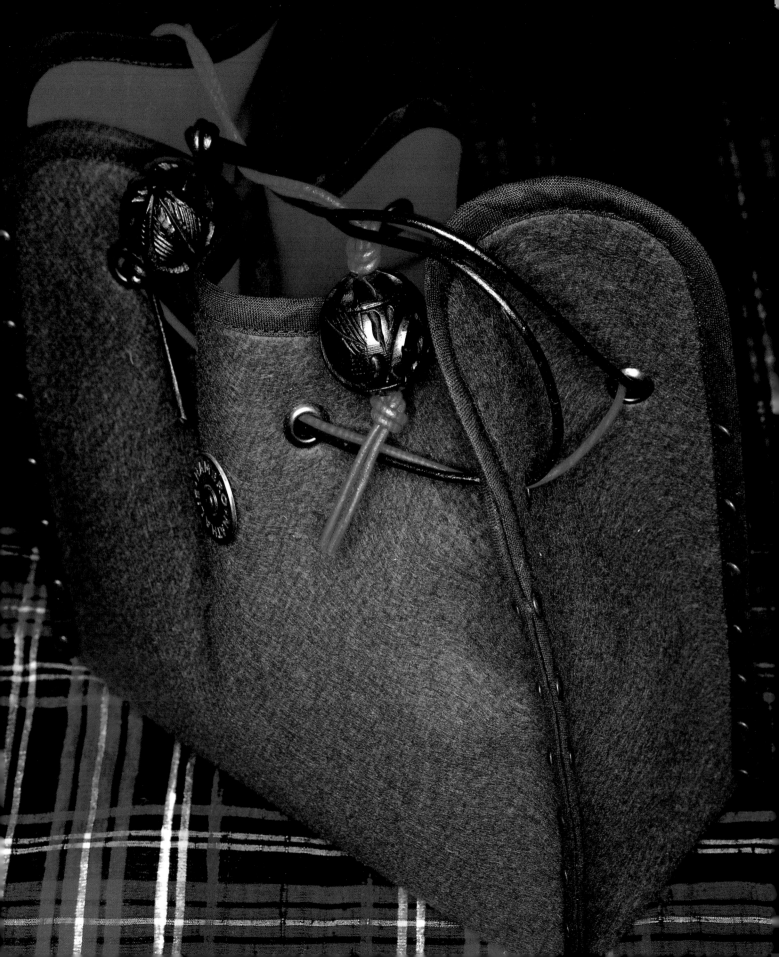

METAL

BUCKET 2 bag,

I made this bag with brass gauze, and decorated it with dashes and dots using different copper powders; I also patinated it with chemicals. The bag has a shot silk lining, the silky cords can be drawn to close the interior lining.

I find developing new techniques rewarding. and I believe in the aesthetic philosophy which says that everything could and should be made beautiful, creating a value system in which all objects large or small, expensive or cheap are of real value.

TRELLIS bag

I used stainless steel gauze for this clutch bag. The trellis is secured with metal buttons and the layered mesh gives an intriguing moiré effect.

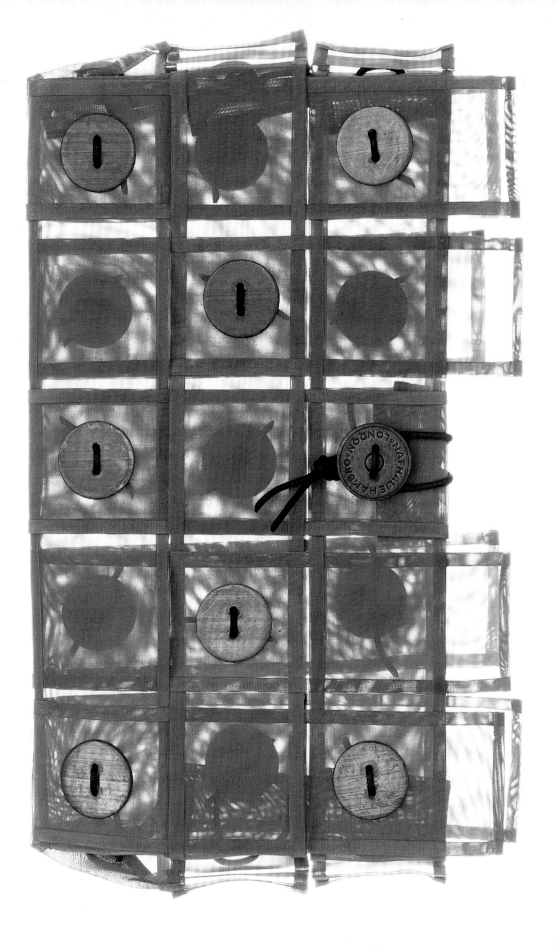

BUCKET 1 bag,

I made this bag reminiscing about childhood holidays. I used stainless steel gauze decorated with enamelled wire squiggles inspired by the interior of a wireless. Hematite beads and grey pearls of various shapes are threaded onto the crimson wire.

INRO bag

Japanese inro were the adornments suspended from the sash of the male traditional costume. These were small scale, often three tiered and closed with a fitted lid. A cord, threaded through two side channels, ties with a toggle. Initially these were containers for seals or medicine, but later became purely sartorial accessories which displayed the lacquer craftsmen's skill.

This is my interpretation of the inrō as a handbag. It is made with stainless steel gauze and embossed lead sheeting. The twisted cord is fashioned from dulled silver threads. The tips of the cord above the toggle are dipped in black sealing wax. I dusted the ribbed toggle bead with powdered metals before lacquering.

X bag,

I constructed the bag from industrial metal . I cut the articulated scales to the desired size and joined the pieces together; criss-crossing the leather cord.

The logo is inspired by a shooting cartridge base and is made from solid silver which I oxidised and polished to a gunmetal finish . The logo is hand-riveted to the bag.

TASSEL bag

For this design I found inspiration from a samurai's ceremonial armour. The bag has an intriguing juxtaposition of textures : sturdy industrial metal flirting with precious silk tasselling. The tassel has a leather double knot on one side and a reef on the other.

FRINGED bag

This bag is my interpretation of a postman's satchel; it is worn over the shoulder and across the chest. The broad strap is made from dyed black jute webbing. The fringe is fashioned with oblong glass beads.

CABAT I bag.

Cabat in French means shopping bag, I wanted to transform an utilitarian day bag into an evening one. I used fine bronze mesh, which I double-folded to finish the edges smooth. The see-through quality of the metal gives it a delicate appearance, although the bag is quite sturdy.

CABAT 2 bag

This is another version of the bronze 'Cabat 1'. The various sections of the bag are tied together with leather cord which is knotted inside; and snipped at an angle to resemble barbed wire.

FABRIC

OBI bag

This bag is inspired by the obi which is the folded sash worn around the waist in traditional Japanese costume. There are as many as five hundred ways to tie the obi; each one takes a different symbolic meaning and gives a sense of occasion; either be casual, festive or ceremonial. The oxidised silver logo pierced with a large hole is reminiscent of an ancient coin.

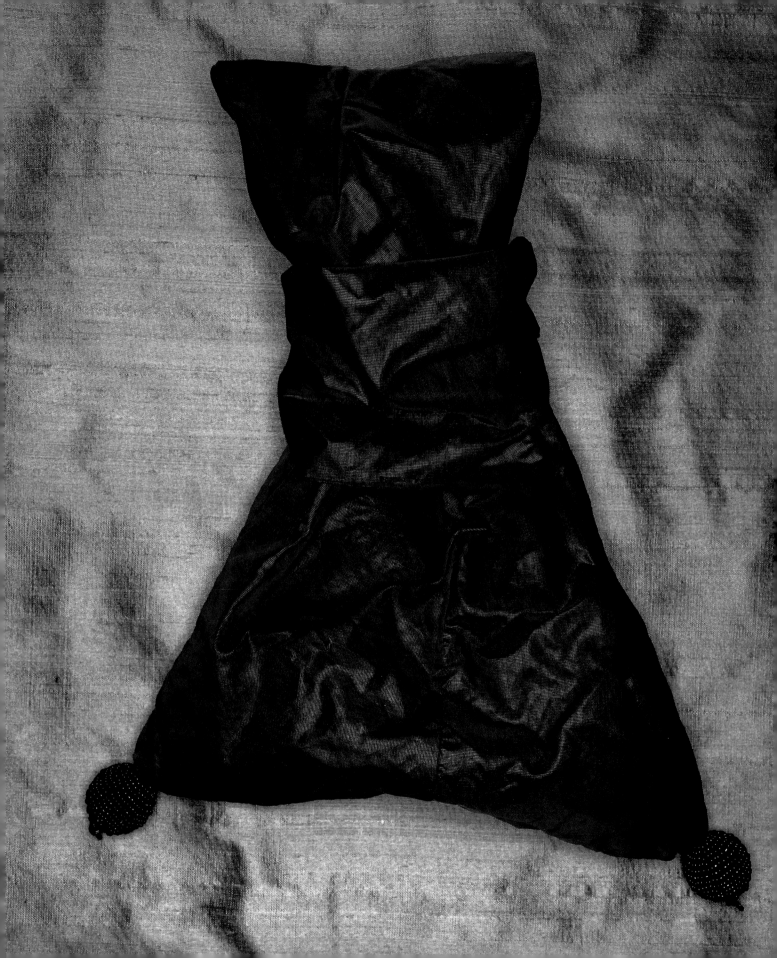

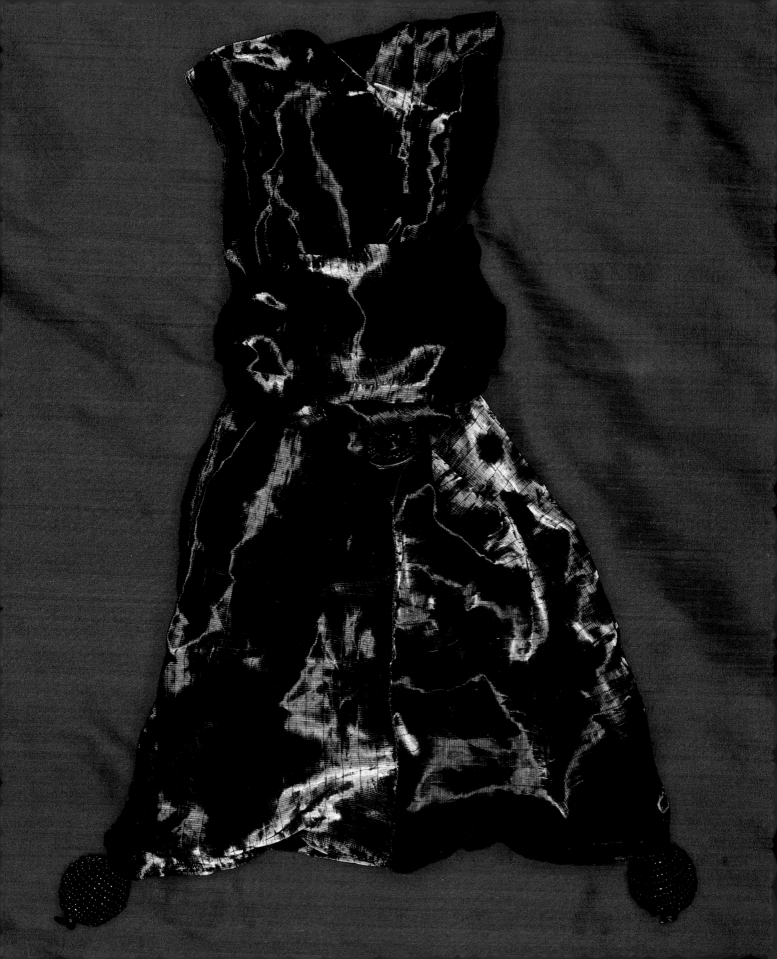

NOH bag.

The kimonos of the Noh theatre were the inspiration behind this design, to this end the bag's lining is as refined and opulent as its exterior. The bag is strengthened with an all around wide horsehair strip.

I have an innate affinity with an Oriental aesthetic and a similar

sense of ritual

which I carry through to any work in my daily life. This rule is even applied to the humblest task, giving me a sense of quality and reward.

There is **rigour** at the

core of my designs, even with

the most opulent ones.

The little

imperfections

of a hand-made bag add a

certain charm that can't be

found in the impersonal

uniformity of a

manufactured one.

TURN-UP bag

I chose for this bag two different antique textiles from Turkestan which are hand-woven on narrow looms. The long bands of fabric are traditionally cut-up to make dresses. The logo is embossed on copper and lacquered.

DRAWSTRING bag

For this bag I used the reverse side of a Chinese silk fabric as it showed a more vibrant combination of colours.
The semi-precious beaded tassels are inspired by 'chao zhu', a Chinese court necklace based on the Buddhist rosary.

PAGODA bag

The pagoda-shaped wooden handles, which are hand-crafted and lacquered, were my starting point for this bag. Its body with lacquered silk which has an unique appearance, somewhere between rubber and leather. The texture is both fluid and sensuous. The intriguing bronzy-black colour is achieved by rubbing the silk with citrus fruit, a revived traditional technique from Vietnam.

WAVE & DOTS SHOES

I worked these shoes with petit-point stitches, the wavy pattern and the dots are both taken from my pencil doodlings. The two feet are similar but not identical: I interverted the design's motifs.

DOUBLE HAPPINESS bag,

For this tapestry bag I used a cross stitch. The free hand design is adapted from an auspicious Chinese symbol which I first saw on a lacquered door in the Forbidden City in Beijing. I chose to work it with silky looking stranded cotton.

The bag is fastened with a metal button embossed with a 'Double Happiness' symbol similar to the one stitched on the tapestry. The intricate 'cloverleaf' knot is my interpretation of one seen in a nineteen century Chinese painting.

PURSE bag

I use horsehair fabric lined with fine felt inside for this small bag. It can either be worn over the wrist, leaving hands free, or on the waist, looped around a belt. Horsehair is woven on old-fashioned looms involving techniques a century old to produce a hard-wearing textile which will last a lifetime.

TOOLS T
OXIDATIOI
RIVETING
DRILLING L
PRESSING
FOLDING
BEN

OOLING

PIERCING

PUNCHING

ACQUERING

CRIMPING

CURVING

DING

I am obsessively fastidious and meticulous over details.

I enjoy the mental conundrum

involved in solving the

construction

of each bag, and the why and

how of every component.

Packaging can have an intrinsic

value quite distinct from its

practical
function.

Style is timeless

The

creative

process

is a convoluted progression

moving forward, while still

looking backwards.

The Team

Photographs: Jonathan Lovekin

Book design: David Eldridge (Senate)

Producer and stylist: Nathalie Hambro

Distribution: Art Books International

Printing: Amica

ACKNOWLEDGEMENTS

SPECIAL THANKS TO: DASHA SHENKMAN WILLIAM SIEGHART ALEXANDRA SHULMAN BARRY SINTON WALTER BOLTON STANLEY KEWICK AND TO: KATIE COWAN CLAIRE DE ROUEN AMY DE LA HAYE JANICE BLACKBURN IAN SHIPLEY MANDREDI DELLA GHERARDESCA DIEGO VON BUCH CHRISTOPHE GOLLUT BALDASSARE LA RIZZA SIMON WALTON